Contents

I'm Ali! Look out for our helpful tips throughout the book.

Hi! I'm Annie and this is my dog, Charlie.

Some words are shown in bold, **like this**. You can find out what they mean by looking in the glossary.

What are disabilities and illnesses?

Everyone gets ill from time to time. But some people have more serious illnesses or disabilities. A disability is a difference that makes it harder for us to do something that others can do easily. Some of us are born with a disability. Others have an illness or injury that causes a disability.

▶ A disability may make it harder for us. But we can still do amazing things.

4

Ali and Annie's Guide to...

Coping with
Illness and
Disability

Jilly Hunt

Raintree is an imprint of Capstone Global Library Limited, a company incorporated in England and Wales having its registered office at 264 Banbury Road, Oxford, OX2 7DY – Registered company number: 6695582

www.raintree.co.uk
myorders@raintree.co.uk

Text © Capstone Global Library Limited 2019
The moral rights of the proprietor have been asserted

Edited by Clare Lewis and Helen Cox Cannons
Designed by Dynamo
Original illustrations © Capstone Global Library Limited 2019
Picture research by Dynamo
Production by Tori Abraham
Originated by Capstone Global Library Limited
Printed and bound in India

ISBN 978 1 4747 7307 2 (hardback)
22 21 20 19 18
10 9 8 7 6 5 4 3 2 1

ISBN 978 1 4747 7313 3 (paperback)
23 22 21 20 19
10 9 8 7 6 5 4 3 2 1

British Library Cataloguing in Publication Data
A full catalogue record for this book is available from the British Library.

Acknowledgements
We would like to thank the following for permission to reproduce photographs:
Alamy: John Fryer, 9; Getty Images: E+/andresr, 19. E+/Dean Mitchell 12, E+/HRAUN, 21, E+/olesiabilkei, 23, E+/PeopleImages, 6, E+/skynesher, 7, E+/SolStock, Cover, 1, E+/Steve Debenport, 10, iStock/FatCamera, 25, 26, 28, iStock/jarenwicklund, 4-5, 27, iStock/monkeybusinessimages, 15, 20, iStock/PaulBiryukov, 22-23, iStock/PeopleImages, 5 Top Right, iStock/Ridofranz, 17, iStock/Sasiistock, 18, iStock/Squaredpixels, 16, iStock/Tijana87, 24, iStock/Wavebreakmedia, 11, 14, iStock/XiXinXing, 13.

We would like to thank Charlotte Mitchell for her invaluable help with the preparation of this book.

Every effort has been made to contact copyright holders of material reproduced in this book. Any omissions will be rectified in subsequent printings if notice is given to the publisher.

▲ This girl has type 1 diabetes. To stay well she has to inject **insulin** into her body every day.

Not all disabilities can be seen. For example, you might not know that someone has **diabetes**, **epilepsy** or deafness. Some people with disabilities take medicine. They may have to go to hospital or doctors regularly.

Why do people get ill?

Many of us get better from illness quite quickly. Some of us get very ill and take a long time to get better. There are lots of causes of illnesses. Some illnesses are called infections. These illnesses are caused by **germs** getting into our bodies.

TIP

By being active and eating well, you can help your body to fight off infections.

Illnesses caused by germs can be spread to other people. When you have a cold, you can spread germs by sneezing.

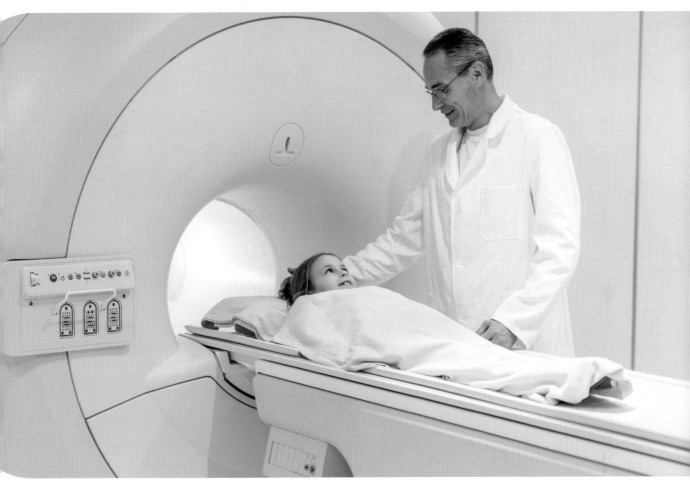

▲ This girl is having a special scan that shows doctors the inside of her body.

Other illnesses can't be spread to other people. These illnesses happen when something in the body changes or stops working properly. Sometimes doctors don't know why we get ill. They have to do lots of tests to try to find out more.

Why do some people have disabilities?

There are many reasons why people have disabilities. Some of us are born with bodies that work differently. Some of us get an illness that changes our lives. Or we might have an injury that will always be with us.

In the UK, the most common disability is difficulty with movement. People might need to use a wheelchair for some or all of the time. Other common disabilities include learning disabilities, and problems with **stamina**, breathing and tiredness.

TIP

Your disability may make you see the world in a different way. Perhaps your behaviour is different from those around you. You might also find it harder to learn things at school.

▶ Tanni Grey-Thompson needs to use a wheelchair every day. She's used it to win 11 Paralympic gold medals and 6 London Marathons.

If you are ill

When you first find out you are ill, you might not know what to feel. You might feel shocked. You might be upset and want to cry. It can feel scary if you don't know what is happening to you.

It can be a confusing time when you find out you are very ill.

Your feelings

Talk to your parents about how you feel. They may be shocked or upset too. You might have lots of questions. Ask your parents if you do. They might not have all the answers. But they can help you find them out.

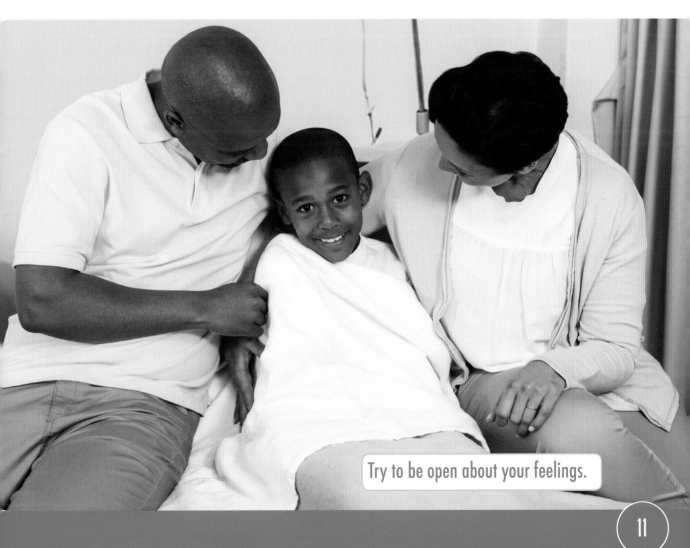

Try to be open about your feelings.

What will happen to me?

You might go to your normal doctor when you are first ill. Or if you are very ill, you may go straight to hospital. A hospital is where people who are ill go to be looked after by doctors and nurses. The doctors may need to do tests on you to find out what is wrong. They may need to give you medicine straight away.

There can be lots of waiting around as the doctor sees other ill people.

Your doctor should tell you what is happening. The doctor might use medical words that you may not have heard before. Tell the doctor if you don't understand something. It can help you feel less worried if you know what is happening.

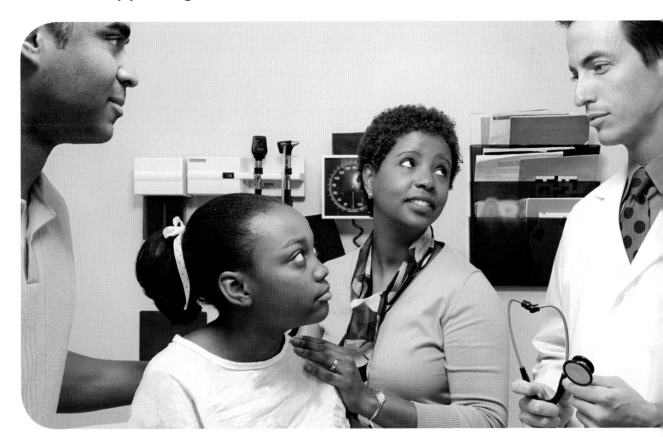

▲ Don't be scared to ask your doctor questions. He or she might not know the answers to everything, though.

What is it like to go to hospital?

An illness can mean that you have to go to hospital to be looked after. Some people have to stay in hospital overnight or for a few days. People who are very ill may need to stay there for a long time.

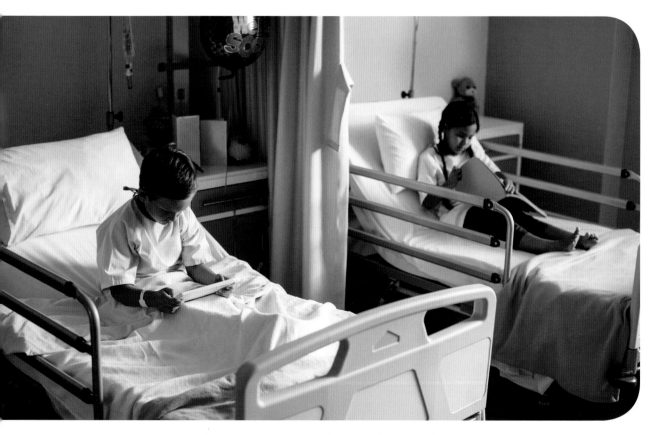

▲ Your hospital bed may be on a **ward** with other children. A parent can usually stay with you. The doctor will come to see you in your bed.

▲ The nurses and doctors are very friendly. They will help you in any way they can.

If you need **treatment** at a hospital you are called a patient. But some patients don't need to stay in hospital to get treatment. They are called day patients. They just visit the hospital for their tests or treatments. Then they go home again.

TIP

If you feel up to it, there may be a room where you can go to play.

If your family member is ill

An ill parent or grandparent

An ill parent or grandparent may mean that things change at home. You may need to stay with other family members or a friend.

Your ill parent or grandparent may sleep more than normal. Sleep helps the body to mend itself.

Your parent or grandparent may need to stay in hospital for a while. They may need treatment that makes them feel ill. They may not have as much energy to play with you.

It's not your fault if you, or somebody you know, is ill. It doesn't mean that you have done something bad or naughty.

▲ You may be able to visit your ill parent or grandparent in hospital.

An ill brother or sister

If you have an ill brother or sister, you may have a mix of feelings. You may be sad or angry that they are ill. A change to your normal routine may make you unsure of what is happening. You might miss your playmate if they are in hospital.

▲ Ask your parents about why your brother or sister is ill. You may be imagining something much worse.

Your parents may need to stay in hospital with your brother or sister. Your parents will probably need to give them extra attention too. This might make you feel a bit jealous of them.

TIP

Try not to feel jealous of the time your parents are giving to your brother or sister. They still love you just as much as before.

You may be able to visit your ill brother or sister in hospital. You could make them a picture to cheer them up.

Living with an illness or disability

Finding out more about your condition will help you to understand it better. You could read books or watch TV programmes about your illness or disability. You might find it helps to learn about other people's experiences.

Finding out how other people live with your condition can help.

Talking to people who have the same illness or disability as you can help too. It's good to talk to someone who understands. Your doctor may be able to put you and your parents in touch with other people who are going through the same thing. Or your parents may be able to find **support groups** on the internet.

It's good to hear other people's stories but remember every body is unique. What has happened to one person might not happen to you, even if you have the same illness or disability.

▲ Knowing more about your condition will help you to feel more in control.

Living with your illness or disability

You may have had your illness or disability for the whole of your life. Or you may be getting used to a different way of living. It can be hard to deal with these changes.

▶ You may find playing with a fidget spinner helps you to calm down.

▲ You might not always feel like talking. You could write your thoughts down or draw a picture to share instead.

Good days and bad days

Nobody has a good day every day. Everyone has challenges to overcome. Living with a disability or illness means you have extra challenges to face. You don't need to pretend that you are happy every day.

It's OK to feel sad about the challenges you face.

If you do have a bad day, don't be hard on yourself. A bad stage doesn't mean that you are not brave or strong. Share your feelings and talk about your worries. Rehearsing any upcoming hospital visits with your parents can help you feel less worried.

TIP

Don't compare yourself with others. Remember, what you see in magazines, on the internet or on TV is not always true. People often show only the good times from their lives.

▲ Ask questions about upcoming doctor's appointments so you know what will happen when you get there.

I can do...

When you are feeling sad, it can be hard to think of anything else. But try not to spend time thinking about what you can't do. Try to think about what you can do instead. Make plans about how to get even better at these things.

Find something that you enjoy doing. It's an extra bonus if you can make friends while doing it.

You might want to challenge yourself to learn a new skill. Break your goals down into small steps. You will see your progress more quickly. You may surprise yourself! Then be proud of your achievement.

You won't know if you can do something unless you give it a try.

TIP

Don't think you can't do something before you even try.

Be proud of who you are

If your illness or disability is new to you, it can take time to get used to it. But you're not on your own. Talk to someone if it starts to feel too much. Your disability is just one part of you. There are lots of other parts too. Be proud of who you are.

Have fun doing what you enjoy!

Ali and Annie's advice

⭐ Doing exercise or playing sport helps you to feel good.

⭐ Eat fruit and vegetables and drink six to eight glasses of water a day.

⭐ Find out as much about your condition as you can.

⭐ Ask questions.

⭐ Don't take your anger or hurt out on other people.

⭐ Find someone you trust to talk to.

⭐ When you feel sad, make plans to look forward to when you feel better.

⭐ Make a list of all the things you can do.

⭐ Keep adding new skills to your list.

⭐ When you try something new, say, "I can do this". If it's harder than you thought, say, "I can't do this yet".

Glossary

diabetes illness that means a person's body has difficulty controlling how much sugar is in their blood. When people have type 1 diabetes, their bodies can't produce the hormone insulin, which helps to control blood sugar.

epilepsy brain condition that makes a person lose consciousness and sometimes have fits (uncontrollable movements)

germ very small living thing that causes disease

insulin hormone produced by the body that controls the amount of glucose in the blood

stamina energy needed to take part in an activity for a long time

support group group run by and for people who have a particular illness or disability

treatment medical care given to a person who is ill

ward large room with lots of beds in a hospital. Patients with similar illnesses and who need similar care from doctors and nurses stay in a ward.

Find out more

Books

Having a Disability (Questions and Feelings About), Louise Spilsbury (Franklin Watts, 2017)

How Are You Feeling Today? Molly Potter (Featherstone, 2014)

No Worries! Katie Abey (Studio Press, 2017)

The Great Big Book of Feelings, Mary Hoffman (Lincoln Children's Books, 2016)

Website

www.childline.org.uk/

The Childline website has support and advice to help you manage your feelings.

Index